Dear Parent:
Your child's love of reading starts here!

Every child learns to read in a different way and at his or her own speed. Some go back and forth between reading levels and read favourite books again and again. Others read through each level in order. You can help your young reader improve and become more confident by encouraging his or her own interests and abilities. From books your child reads with you to the first books he or she reads alone, there are I Can Read Books for every stage of reading:

SHARED READING
Basic language, word repetition, and whimsical illustrations, ideal for sharing with your emergent reader

BEGINNING READING
Short sentences, familiar words, and simple concepts for children eager to read on their own

READING WITH HELP
Engaging stories, longer sentences, and language play for developing readers

READING ALONE
Complex plots, challenging vocabulary, and high-interest topics for the independent reader

ADVANCED READING
Short paragraphs, chapters, and exciting themes for the perfect bridge to chapter books

I Can Read Books have introduced children to the joy of reading since 1957. Featuring award-winning authors and illustrators and a fabulous cast of beloved characters, I Can Read Books set the standard for beginning readers.

A lifetime of discovery begins with the magical words "I Can Read!"

Visit www.icanread.ca for information
on enriching your child's reading experience.

I Can Read Book® is a trademark of HarperCollins Publishers

Hayley's Journey
Text copyright © 2019 by HarperCollins Publishers Ltd.
Illustrations © 2019 by Nick Craine.
All rights reserved. Published by Collins, an imprint of HarperCollins Publishers Ltd

This work is adapted from the story "Hayley Wickenheiser, Hockey Legend" in *5-Minute Stories for Fearless Girls* by Sarah Howden, illustrations by Nick Craine.
No part of this book may be used or reproduced in any manner whatsoever without the prior written permission of the publisher, except in the case of brief quotations embodied in reviews.

HarperCollins books may be purchased for educational, business, or sales promotional use through our Special Markets Department.

HarperCollins Publishers Ltd
Bay Adelaide Centre, East Tower
22 Adelaide Street West, 41st Floor
Toronto, Ontario, Canada
M5H 4E3

www.harpercollins.ca

Library and Archives Canada Cataloguing in Publication information is available upon request.

www.icanread.ca

ISBN 978-1-4434-5733-0

WZL   1 2 3 4 5 6 7 8 9 10

I Can Read!

READING 2 WITH HELP

HAYLEY'S JOURNEY

by Sarah Howden

Illustrations by Nick Craine

Collins

Hayley Wickenheiser

is seven years old.

She is skating on the ice rink

in her backyard.

It is late at night.

Hayley doesn't mind the dark.

She can feel where the puck is.

She can hear where it's going.

Hayley's dad comes outside.

"What are you doing?" he asks.

"It's pitch-black out here!"

Hayley knows he's not mad.

She can tell that he's smiling.

"I couldn't sleep," Hayley says

with a shrug.

Then she turns and shoots the puck.

Hayley is now ten.

She is on a boys' hockey team.

"I'm just as good as any boy,"

she says as she laces her skates.

But Hayley is a girl.

It can be hard being different

from her teammates.

"I think I'll tuck my hair up,"
Hayley says.

"Then no one will know the truth."

Hayley hopes that one day
it won't matter that she's a girl.
She hopes it will be easier
to just play the game she loves.

Hayley moves the puck down the ice.

She is quick and strong.

"Good work!" says her coach.

Hayley nods and shoots the puck.

Hayley works hard over the years.
She trains at the rink and
she trains at home.

And one day she makes it

to Team Canada.

Hayley is only fifteen years old.

Team Canada is about to play

the gold-medal game.

"Can I do this?" Hayley wonders.

Hayley looks around at the
other women on her team.
She used to dream of
playing with them.

"You are my heroes," Hayley says.

They smile at her.

"Maybe one day I'll be a hero too,"

she thinks.

Then the game begins.

Now Hayley only thinks about

playing her best.

Hayley takes a deep breath.

And she shoots the puck.

Now Hayley is all grown up.

She is on Canada's

Olympic hockey team.

Hayley has been to the

Olympics before.

But this time is special.

This year the Olympics

are in Canada.

And Hayley is the team captain.

Team Canada has made it to

the final game.

They will play against Team USA.

Both teams are great.

Either team could win gold.

The game is about to start.

"We can do this!"

Hayley calls to her team.

The crowd roars from the stands.

Hayley gets ready.

The puck is dropped.

"I've got it!" Hayley calls.

The game is on!

Hayley has worked hard to get here.

It's been a long journey.

"We're going to win this game,"

Hayley thinks to herself.

And Hayley is right!

Team Canada wins gold.

Hayley is a true hero.

She always has been.